CLARENCE TALLEY SR.

Jesus Christ
Made Straight A's:
STUDY QUESTIONS

AUCTOREM
H O U S E

Auctorem House
276 5th Ave, Ste 704-2591
New York, NY 10001
www.auctoremhouse.com
1.888.332.7718

To
The Mount

CONTENTS

THE CLASSROOM OF CHRIST

This booklet is meant to accompany the book: Jesus Christ Made Straight A's. It is a study in the Word of God with thought provoking questions and analyses.

As Jesus Christ humbled Himself in the classroom of life to accomplish the will of the Father, we must do the same. His perfect submission is our perfect example. His life is the grand pattern to which we are called to follow. To do so, we must turn our attention to the Bible. We must study to show ourselves approved unto God by seeking His truths found only in the His Word.

CHAPTER 1

JESUS MADE
STRAIGHT A'S

1. In what ways does this period in Jesus's life interest or bless you? How is it important to you?

2. As a child, were you required to bring home good grades (A's and B's), or were you told to "just do your best"?

3. What expectations would a parent of school-age children have for those children?

4. The Bible is silent regarding Jesus's life from the time He went back to Nazareth after His first Passover (at the age of 12) until we see Him again coming to John the Baptist to be baptized. Regarding those early years, William Barclay[1] states that:

---

[1] William Barclay, *Gospel of Matthew Vol. 1: The Years Between*, pp. 40-43.

i. Jesus was growing up to boyhood, and then to manhood, in a good home; there can be no greater start to life than that.

ii. Jesus was fulfilling the duties of an eldest son. It seems most likely that Joseph died before the children grew up. Maybe he was already much older than Mary when they married. In the story of the Wedding Feast at Cana of Galilee, there is no mention of Joseph, although Mary is there, and it is natural to suppose that Joseph had died. So Jesus became the village craftsman of Nazareth to support his mother and his younger brothers and sisters. A world was calling him, and yet he first fulfilled his duty to his mother and to his own folks and to his own home. Jesus is the great example of one who accepted the simple duties of the home.

iii. Jesus was learning what it was like to be a working man. He was learning what it was like to have to earn a living; to save to buy food and clothes, and maybe sometimes a little pleasure; to meet the dissatisfied and the critical customer, and the customer who would not pay his debts. If Jesus was to help men, he must first know what men's lives were like. He did not come into a protected cushioned life; he came into the life that any man must live. He had to do that if he was ever to understand the life of ordinary people.

Have you ever wondered about those years? Explain.

5. When does a Jewish boy become a *child of the Law*? What does it mean to become a *child of the Law*?

6. In John 1:45-46, it states that Jesus's hometown of Nazareth had a bad reputation. Why? What kind of reputation does your hometown have?

7. Why did it take three days for Joseph and Mary to find Jesus once they discovered He was not with the caravan headed back to Nazareth?

8. Have you ever been misplaced or left behind by accident or intentionally?

9. What is the "blame game"? Husbands and wives, friends and enemies do it often. Have you ever played the blame game? Explain.

10. The boy Jesus was an *attentive* listener. Later in His ministry, listening played an important part, and He warned others of its necessity. (The phrase appears seven times in the gospels and seven times in Revelation 2-3 [see Matthew 11:14-15]. In addition, see Matthew 13:9, Mark 4:9, and Luke 8:8, where the subject is the Sower, as well as Mark 4:23, Mark 7:16, and Luke 14:35.) What was Jesus's favorite phraseology when warning others to listen?

11. Who enlightened the boy Jesus about the characteristics of the Father? (Isaiah 50:4-5)

12. What great thinkers/teachers were likely present when the boy Jesus visited the Temple?

13. Solomon had much to say about listening. What does he say about a wise man in Proverbs 1:5?

14. Jesus earned His first "A" for _____.

15. A prized method of teaching was that of _____ and.

16. What was Socrates's method of teaching?

17. Jesus earned His second "A" for _____.

18. We do not know what questions Jesus may have asked, nor do we know what specific answers and responses He had to various questions. Those who heard Him, however, were at His responses. (Luke 2:46-47)

19. What was Joseph and Mary's response when they found Him conversing with doctors and lawyers? (Luke 2:48a)

20. In discussions, asking questions is important. We do not know what questions Jesus put to those gathered in the Temple, but He did ask questions. After Jesus began His ministry, the questions He asked played an important part in expanding understanding and getting listeners to think. For example, Jesus asked:

   • "Do you believe that I am able to do this?" (Matt. 9:28)
   • "Why are you afraid, O you of little faith?" (Matt. 8:26)

- "What do you think about the Christ?" (Matt. 22:42)
- "Do you love Me?" (John 21:17)
- "Why do you call Me 'Lord, Lord,' and not do what I tell you?" (Luke 6:46)
- "What do you want Me to do for you?" (Luke 18:41)
- "Why do you see the speck that is in your brother's eye, but do not notice the log that is in your own eye?" (Matt. 7:3)

Using the list above, choose which questions asked by Jesus stir your spiritual interest. Why?

21. At an early age, Jesus felt compelled to be about "_____."

22. After the Passover experience, Jesus returned to Nazareth with His parents and grew "_____."

23. Jesus was baptized by _____ in the

24. Jesus's mission was to bridge _____ the between God and _____.

25. What does Jesus's wilderness experience teach us about our daily struggle with temptations?

26. What temptations do you face? Are our temptations any more difficult or different from Jesus's temptations? (See 1 Corinthians 10:13).

27. Why was Jesus seemingly reluctant to get involved in handling the shortage of wine?

28. What did Jesus mean by "Mine hour is not yet come"? (John 2:4).

29. The testimony of the master of the ceremony in John 2:10 was that the wine was the best he had tasted and was surely deserving of an _____.

30. According to Matthew 4:23-24, what are the basic components of Jesus's ministry?

31. What did the common people say when they testified about the quality of Jesus's teaching? (See Matthew 7:29)

32. Luke 4:18-20 summarizes Jesus's mission and ministry. Is there a primary text, Bible story, or Biblical character that has helped shape your ministry (service) and mission in life?

33. What incident occurred that earned Jesus an "A" in writing?

34. What did Jesus do to earn an "A" in science?

35. Reading, writing, arithmetic, physics, and science are the subjects in which Jesus excelled. In studying His life, what other areas of importance do you find that He excelled in? Love? Forgiveness? Caring? Counseling? Others? Cite one scriptural example for each topic.

36. What did Jesus mean by us, His disciples, doing greater things?

CHAPTER 2
HOW TO MAKE GOD'S HONOR ROLL

1. What does it take to make God's honor roll?

2. On a scale of 1-10, 10 being the highest, how smart would you say you are?

3. What Scriptures, sermons, or sage advice have you received that caused you to really believe in yourself?

4. How do you register for the classroom of Jesus Christ?

5. Courses in the classroom of Christ are not free. How were they paid for?

6. In the classroom of Christ, how does Jesus achieve individualized instruction?

7. According to Scriptures, how is honor obtained?

8. Honor "by God" is obtained by _____ Jesus Christ.

9. What are the qualifications of a Godly servant?

10. Spiritual service for Jesus Christ is carried out by followers of Christ on behalf of _____.

11. What is meant by "no following, no serving"?

12. Explain John 12:23-26. What is Jesus's "hour"?

13. As first fruit of the dead, Jesus became the Captain of our _____.

14. Complete allegiance is commanded by God. What sets us at odds with God? (See James 4:4)

15. What is God's invitation to His faithful servants? (See Matthew 25:34)

16. Interpret the following quote from Dr. Martin L. King, Jr.: "Everybody can be great. Because everybody can serve."

CHAPTER 3

THE BOOMERANG OF DECEIT: DANIEL AND HIS CO-WORKERS

1. Have you experienced jealousy, envy, or criticism from co-workers, family members, church members, or friends because God has blessed and continues to bless you?

2. Where does promotion come from? (Psalm 75:6)

3. If your background were checked, what would be discovered? Have you been living for the Master or the world? (See Daniel 6:4)

4. Is your commitment to God widely known among men?

5. How did Daniel respond to the trap his co-workers set?

6. Daniel's custom was to pray three times a day. What is your custom? (Daniel 6:10)

7. What does the name Daniel mean?

8. What does Psalm 37:1-2 tell us about evildoers?

9. Did Daniel resist the officers when they arrived to arrest him? What did the officers find Daniel doing?

10. What key ingredient is needed when facing our own lion's den?

11. In times of difficulty, why is it so important to turn everything over to God?

12. What does a loving relationship with God mean to you?

13. What assurances do Psalm 91:11 and Psalm 34:7 reveal?

14. According to Hebrews 11:34, what "stopped the mouths of lions"?

15. Vengeance, retribution, and recompense all belong to _____.

16. What does the "law of reciprocity" teach?

17. What happened to the men who falsely accused Daniel? (Daniel 6:24)

18. What is the fate of those who plot evil?

19. Explain the phrase "the consequences of sin know no respect of person."

20. God is awesome. How is He awesome in your life? (A Testimony)

CHAPTER 4

FROM MASTER CHEF TO RESTORER

1. List three occasions where we find Jesus dining with others.

   a. _____

   b. _____

   a. _____

2. What master artists painted the holy event called The Last Supper?

3. The complaint by the Pharisees and scribes about Jesus eating with publicans and sinners led to the telling of and _____, two of the greatest parables ever told (Luke 15).

4. What would be a "balanced meal" from the Master Chef? (See 2 Timothy 3:16)

5. Though Peter failed Jesus, it was Peter who identified Jesus as
   _____. (Matthew 16:16)

6. Jesus predicted that Peter would deny Him _____
   times. (Matthew 26:34)

7. In the life of the believer, failure will occur either by
   _____ or by _____.

8. When we have sinned, what should we do? (1 John 1:9)

9. In Psalm 51, "a cry of restoration" by David, what did David
   petition God to do and not do? (See Psalm 51:10-12)

10. Peter's restoration could only be done in _____.
    (Ephesians 4:32)

11. _____ is the glue that binds all hearts.
    _____ is the glue that mends shattered faith and
    fractured dreams.

12. Can anything separate us from the love of God? (Romans 8:35)

13. The Master Chef fed the disciples both spiritual and physical
    food. After that, what did He command Peter to do?

14. When Peter expressed concern to Jesus about the destiny of
    John, how did Jesus respond? (See John 21:20-24)

15. Our participation in kingdom building must be predicated on our _____ with God.

16. Following Jesus means we must keep our eyes on _____ , focus on the job He has assigned _____ , and stay _____ of the affairs of others.

CHAPTER 5

THE MISTREATMENT OF JESUS CHRIST

1. What is the best way to relate to others? (See Matthew 22:37-39)

2. What is the bedrock of interpersonal relations?

3. When there is _____ or no _____ for God, it is easy to mistreat others.

4. The root cause of sin against others is a lack of _____ for God.

5. Define "righteous anger."

6. Name-calling has always been a tool of the enemy. What were some of the names Jesus's opponents used to denigrate Him?

7. What common courtesies have slowly become verbal dinosaurs?

8. Were all of the Pharisees enemies of Jesus?

9. Have you ever been invited to an occasion where you were not truly welcome, yet you accepted the invitation?

10. Why should we abstain from judging others and from drawing firm conclusions about others? (Romans 3:23; 1 Corinthians 13:12a)

11. What was the Pharisees' summation concerning Jesus and the woman? (Luke 7:36-39)

12. What does Matthew 7:3-4 teach about judging others?

13. When did Jesus address the Pharisees' mistreatment of Him?

14. What is the Old Testament perspective on the treatment of strangers, widows, the fatherless, and the motherless? (Deuteronomy 16:11, 24:17-22; Jeremiah 7:6)

15. What does Hebrews 13:2 say about entertaining strangers?

16. What we think is important to God because we are who we are from the _____. (Proverbs 23:7; Ephesians 4:8)

17. What is Solomon's warning regarding discussions that take place in our heart? (Proverb 4:23)

18. Why is God's judgment of us not superficial? (1 Samuel 16:7)

19. Our sensitivity to the saving work of Jesus Christ should motivate us to _____, _____ and _____.

CHAPTER 6

HOSEA AND GOMER: A PORTRAIT OF GOD'S LOVE

1. Whose idea was it that Hosea marry Gomer (see Hosea 1:2)? Why?

2. How was God using Hosea and Gomer's marriage? (Hosea 1:2b)

3. What was the name of Hosea's first child? What does the name mean?

4. What does Exodus 20:1-5 tell us about Yahweh?

5. What was the name of Hosea's second child? Third child?

6. What is the significance of the names, as given by God?

7. What did the removal of "Lo" in each name reveal?

8. What had Hosea done to cause Gomer to walk out on the prophet?

9. To assist the prophet with his dire situation, he was to solicit the help of the _____.

10. Symbolically, Gomer represented _____ and Hosea represented _____.

11. We can _____ our children by our actions, and we can our children by our actions.

12. Who do Hosea's children represent?

13. What did the Lord threaten to do to Gomer (Israel) in Hosea 2:3-4?

14. What did Gomer say in crediting her lovers with her well-being? (Hosea 2:5, 8)

15. Who were Israel's lovers?

16. Why did Hosea take Gomer back? (Hosea 3:1)

17. What did Hosea have to do to get Gomer back? (Hosea 3:2a)

18. What is the worst mistake we can make in life?

19. What did our redemption cost God? (John 3:16; 1 Corinthians 6:19-20, 7:23)

20. After purchasing Gomer back, what did Hosea require of her? (Hosea 3:3)

21. _____ is an example of God's jealousy, judgment, love, and forgiveness.

22. What is the most famous portrait in the entire world?

23. Why did Israel fail to recognize the love of God in the life of the nation? (Hosea 4:6, 5:5, 6:4)

24. God knows when our goodness is _____ and when our worship is _____. (John 4:24)

25. God commands that we worship Him in spirit and truth, not, _____ or _____.

26. How did Hosea describe the coming destruction upon Israel? (Hosea 8:7)

27. God's portrait of love was painted on the canvas of _____.

28. God's grand portrait of love is our _____ to return to God.

CHAPTER 7

"BE COOL, I GOT THIS"

1. The Lord will not be mocked by man with.

2. At the appointed time, the wicked will get what they _____.

3. In our response to evil, we are told not to be _____, _____, or _____.

4. God will _____ because God does not _____.

5. What five commands are given in Psalm 37:3-8?

6. Just as God commands our faithfulness in Psalm 37:3-8, He also _____ the evildoers to turn from their wicked ways (See Psalm 37:27 and Amos 5:14).

7. Faith is of God. Fear is from the _____. (2 Timothy 1:7)

8. What did Moses tell the people as they stood frightened before the Red Sea? (Exodus 14:13-14)

9. To set in motion God's plan of deliverance, what was Moses asked to do in Exodus 14:16?

10. Exodus 14 teaches that there is nothing _____, or _____ with God.

11. What are some of our present-day Red Seas?

12. How does God respond to our present-day Red Seas?

13. Why did the Hebrew boys feel they did not need to defend themselves? (Also see Daniel 3:16-18)

14. What comfort could the Hebrew boys get from Isaiah 43:2 and Psalm 46:1?

15. What arrogant statement was spoken by King Nebuchadnezzar in Daniel 3:15?

16. The Hebrew boys were accompanied in the fiery furnace by

_____.

17. In time, God will bring us out of the furnace of this
_____ world.

18. Upon their exit from the fiery furnace, what condition were the Hebrew boys in? (Daniel 3:27)

19. Job 14:1 makes it plain that there will be storms in our lives. What are the present weather conditions in your life? (Clear skies, thunderstorms, hurricane, intermittent showers, etc.)

20. We can make it through the storms of life when we "walk by _____." (1 Corinthians 5:7)

21. Materially, Job lost everything, but to make matters worse, Job's seven _____ and three _____ were killed.

22. What was Job's response to the storms in his life? (Job 1:20-21)

23. Why did Satan want to afflict Job's body?

24. Job's wife gave her husband the wrong advice (Job 2:9). How do we avoid such a mistake?

25. What was Job's response to his wife? (Job 2:10)

26. How did Job's friends who had come to visit him respond when they saw him? (Job 2:12)

27. After seeing Job and conversing with him, what did Job's friends conclude? Was their assessment correct?

28. Were Job's friends of any consolation to him? (Job 13:4, 16:2)

29. Though Job wanted an audience with God, did Job, or do we, have a right to demand answers from God? (Job 23:3-4, 38:2)

30. Can man rightfully demand anything from God? (Romans 9:20, Psalms 100:3)

31. God will always do what is right, whether we _____ His actions or not.

32. What were some of the errors Job made in wanting to confront God? (Job 40:2, 40:8, 42:3)

33. After realizing God had his situation under control, what did Job resign to do? (Job 40:4-5)

34. Job was awarded _____ for his troubles. God restored unto Job _____, _____, _____, and _____. (Job 42:11b, 13, 14, 16-17)

35. As long as the Lord is on the _____ and the _____, we have no need to worry and no need to fear.

CHAPTER 8

CONFESSION
IS GOOD FOR
THE SOUL

1. Because God knows our transgressions, it is wise to _____,
    _____.

2. What is God willing to do if we confess our sins? (1 John 1:9)

3. An unwillingness to acknowledge sin does not mean.

4. In Joshua 7, Achan carried out his sin under the guise that
    _____, _____, and as a result, everything would
    be all right.

5. What were the forbidden treasures Achan took for himself?

6. What was the result of Achan's sin?

7. What judgment did Achan bring on himself and his family? (Joshua 7:24-25)

8. What were King David's notable sins?

9. What was David's initial plan to deceive Bathsheba's husband?

10. Why did King David's plan to deceive Uriah not work?

11. When Plan B did not work, King David resorted to what? (2 Samuel 11:14-17)

12. According to 2 Samuel 11:27, how did God feel about King David's actions?

13. After his tryst with Bathsheba, was King David content with his secret sins? (Psalm 32:3-4)

14. Whom did God send to confront King David about his sins? How did the prophet confront the king?

15. What was the king's initial response to Nathan's parable?

16. Nathan confronted David in a spirit of _____ and _____.

17. What is Paul's warning to us as we confront fellow Christians about their sin(s)?

18. What was King David's confession to Nathan?

19. How did the prophet summarize the consequences of King David's sins?

20. What do Deuteronomy 30:15-19 and Galatians 6:7 teach about the consequences of sin?

21. Hindsight and foresight are important. How does the Bible help us in these areas?

22. When we sow the wind, we will reap a _____. (Hosea 8:7)

23. What problems did King David face within his household?

24. What did King David do when faced with the eminent death of the child born to the king and Bathsheba? (2 Samuel 12:14-23)

25. How does God respond to our prayers?

26. What act did Anhithophel encourage Absalom, the son of David, to commit against his father? (2 Samuel 12:11-13; 2 Samuel 21-22)

27. What was the fiasco between Amnon, his half-sister Tamar, and Absalom? (2 Samuel 12:11-13)

28. If we sow to the flesh, we shall _____ the flesh.

29. Psalm 51 is King David's psalm of confession. Have you ever turned to it for consolation?

CHAPTER 9

CAN I BE ALL GOD WANTS ME TO BE?

1. The void in man's heart constantly reminds us that "_____."

2. Why did Abraham and Sarah question their ability to bear a child?

3. What was Moses's reluctance in accepting God's call?

4. Why was Jeremiah, who was preordained to be "a prophet to the nations," faithless?

5. What was Isaiah's opinion of himself that caused him to question his abilities?

6. Contrast Zechariah, the priest, with Mary, the future mother of the Messiah. How do they differ?

7. _____ denied Jesus three times, yet God could still use him. (John 21:15-17)

8. _____was warned: "It is not good to kick against the prick."

9. _____ is the Supreme Believer in us becoming all that He has ordained us to be; however, too often.

10. How do we know we can do "great things" for the Lord? (John 14:12; Ephesians 3:20)

11. List the three reasons why we can be all God wants us to be.
    a. _____
    b. _____
    c. _____

12. How does Romans 8:28 assure us that God wants us to be all that we can be?

13. What plans does God have for all our lives? (Jeremiah 29:11)

14. How does our free will play a role in us becoming all God wants us to be?

15. Accepting the gift of _____ is foundational to becoming all you can be.

16. A life totally submitted to God will release its _____, and _____ to Him.

17. No one can be all God wants them to be without being guided by His _____.

18. What must we *know, believe,* and *accept* beyond a shadow of a doubt?

19. When seeking answers to whatever may come our way, the right source is "_____."

20. How does the Psalmist describe the Word of God in Psalm 19?

21. For our faith to grow, believers must submit by _____ to the _____.

22. Read Matthew 5-7, commonly known as the Sermon on the Mount. Is there a particular teaching that speaks to you loud and clear?

23. Satan may impede you or slow you down, but he is incapable of completely derailing what God has _____.

24. The power to be all we can be lies with _____.

25. Equipped with the whole armor of God, Satan cannot exercise and _____ over us.

26. What is Satan's destiny?

CHAPTER 10

JUST WAIT

1. Waiting requires _____, _____, and _____.

2. Match the following examples of waiting:

   The Church   A. Congregant to mature
   Mothers-to-be   B. Free of parental restrictions
   Teachers   C. Jesus's return
   Parents   D. For the seed to germinate
   Pastors   E. Students to master skills
   Children   F. Children to mature
   Farmers   G. The nine-month journey

3. Impatience can be _____, _____, and even _____.

4. What did Sarah suggest that Abraham do to hurry along God's plan? (Genesis 16:1-6)

5. What blessing did Moses forfeit because of impatience and disobedience? (Numbers 20:10-12)

6. The Israelites' impatience with Moses as he spent 40 days on Mount Sinai caused them to make a _____. (Exodus 32)

7. Job's wife's impatience caused her to flippantly encourage her husband to "_____ God and die." (Job 2:9)

8. James and John became so impatient with the Samaritans that they asked Jesus for permission to call _____ down on a Samaritan village. (Luke 9:51-56)

9. We must guard against the temptation to act when waiting is _____.

10. When Jesus was tempted to act in John 2:4, how did He respond?

11. Jesus is the perfect picture of _____.

12. Why, from God's vantage point, is it important that waiting be done?

13. Psalm 27:14 commands that believers "_____," and in the process of waiting, "_____," and as a result God will "_____."

14. What are some of the specific circumstances in Psalm 27 in which believers may have to wait?

15. What does it mean to be of "good courage"?

16. How did Job wait on the Lord? (Job 13:15, 14:14)

17. Patience in the pits of life guarantees the _____ and _____ by God.

18. What makes waiting worthwhile?

19. What is the benefit of waiting according to Isaiah 40:29?

20. What three things can the believer be assured of according to Isaiah 40:31b?

    a. _____

    b. _____

    c. _____

21. How is Isaiah 40:31b seen as a picture of life?

22. Our duty is to wait, but HOW?

    _____ Wait Continually   A. Lamentations 3:26
    _____ Wait Expectantly   B. Psalm 25:4-5
    _____ Wait Prayerfully   C. Psalm 62:5-6
    _____ Wait Quietly   D. Hosea 12:6

CHAPTER 11

HIS NAME SHALL BE CALLED

1. What question did Jesus ask His disciples regarding Himself? (Matthew 16:13)

2. What was the disciples' answer to Jesus's question?

3. Who gave the answer that pleased Jesus? What did that disciple say?

4. How did Jesus describe Himself? Son of _____, _____ , and _____.

5. How did others describe Jesus?

6. The first specific mention of Jesus Christ in Scripture is found in _____. He is described as _____ of woman.

7. What names are attributed to the Christ child in Isaiah 9:6?

8. The *how* of the Immaculate Conception was explained to Mary by the angel _____.

9. The wonderful birth of Jesus caused angels to appear and declare what?

10. The wonderful childhood of Jesus is seen in the fact that He grew in _____ and _____.

11. Though betrayed, denied, and abandoned by His disciples, Jesus was still _____.

12. Jesus was wonderful in His post-resurrection _____.

13. After His death, burial, and resurrection, Jesus received a wonderful _____ from Thomas: _____

14. Jesus's power-walk on the road to Emmaus, His restoration of Peter, His commission of the disciples, His ascension, and His Second Coming all illustrate how _____ and magnificent our Lord and Savior is.

15. Unlike human counselors, Jesus is both _____ Son of man and _____ Son of God.

16. Jesus is the solution to every _____.

17. What is the warning in Proverbs 21:30 (NIV)?

18. Jesus Christ, the Counselor, is the personification of _____, _____, and _____. (Isaiah 40:28; Proverbs 8:14)

19. Jesus Christ, the Counselor, only speaks the _____.

20. Jesus Christ, the Counselor, only says what _____ the Father. (John 8:29)

21. Jesus's counseling/teaching was unlike others. He taught as one having _____. (Matthew 7:29)

22. Jesus Christ's counseling is relevant and reliable, _____, _____, and _____.

23. Match the following:

THE COUNSELED   THE COUNSELING

    Nicodemus   A. "Obedience is better than sacrifice."

    The Disciples   B. "It's hard to kick against the prick."

    King Saul   C. "You must be born again."

Saul	D. "Do what you must do and do it quickly."
Peter	E. "I am the resurrection and the life."
Judas	F. "Feed My Sheep."
Martha	G. "Go and make disciples."

24. The Hebrew *El Shaddai* means.

25. What question did God ask Job that attests to His power and majesty?

26. The most memorable example of the *might* of God is seen in the parting of the _____.

27. The invincibility of God is seen when one angel of the Lord killed _____ Assyrian soldiers in one night.

28. The orchestration of the redemption of man could only be achieved by _____.

29. The might of the Master was demonstrated throughout His earthly ministry. Give three examples.

    a. _____

    b. _____

    c. _____

30. "The everlasting Father" is a name full of _____.

31. What does it mean to say that God is "from everlasting to everlasting"? (Psalm 90:2)

32. Jesus spoke of His everlasting state of being in Revelation 1:8 and Revelation 11. How did He describe Himself?

33. God is the everlasting Father of all _____. In addition, He is the spiritual, everlasting Father of all who have experienced a _____.

34. How was the idea of the *new birth* declared to Nicodemus? (John 3:7)

35. How is the *love* of the everlasting Father revealed toward man? (John 3:16)

36. Because God is "The everlasting Father," we can look forward to _____.

37. What will characterize Jesus's earthly kingdom?

38. Did Christ bring peace during His first advent? (Luke 1:79)

39. How did those of Jesus's day respond to His way of peace?

40. The refusal of true contentment (peace) always leads to and _____. (Matthew 10:34-36)

41. Jesus's light, love, and life were rejected because men's deeds are essentially _____. (John 3:19)

42. Evil (Satan) prefers reigning in hell rather than serving in _____.

43. How have we received peace from The Prince of Peace?

44. How do we have the peace of God? (Romans 5:1)

CHAPTER 12

WHAT GOD EXPECTS

1. Have those around you (family members, friends, acquaintances) shared their expectations of you with you?

2. Match the following expectations that one group has for another:

    Athletes   A. Principals
    Citizens   B. Fathers
    Businesses   C. Pastors
    Employees   D. Customers
    Teachers   E. Coaches
    Sons   F. Employers
    Congregations   G. Governments

3. Questions of a spiritual nature must be answered by closely the Word of God.

4. What is the legacy of the Bereans? (Acts 17:11)

5. What did God expect of Adam and Eve?

6. What warning was given to Adam? (Genesis 2:16-17)

7. What did God expect of Moses? (Exodus 3:10)

8. What did God expect of the Levitical priest?

9. What did God expect the Hebrews to do in the book of Numbers?

10. In the book of Deuteronomy, what did God expect of His people as they prepared to enter the land of milk and honey?

11. Are we living up to the expectations of God in light of the Old Testament historical examples? (See 1 Corinthians 10:1-11)

12. According to God's expectation, how do you understand Psalm 119:89?

13. What are we commanded to do in Luke 10:19?

14. Living up to God's expectations always bring _____; disobedience always nets _____.

15. In the Old Testament, what passage singularly summed up what Jehovah expected of Israel?

16. In Micah 6:3-5, what did God want to know?

17. To do justly is to do _____.

18. The concept of *doing justly* (the Old Testament) is summed up in _____. (Matthew 7:12)

19. A lover of mercy is a person of _____.

20. What is promised in Matthew 5:7?

21. _____ with God is predicated upon being just and merciful.

22. According to the New Testament, what scripture(s) sums up God's expectation of man?

23. James 1:27 teaches that _____ toward others and living a _____ is what God expects.

24. Matthew 23:23 teaches us to place more emphasis on judgment, _____, and to _____.

25. What had the Pharisees and scribes replaced for "the weightier matters of the Law"?

26. What does man owe God and man? (John 13:34-35, Romans 13:8)

27. We are to love God with our _____, _____, _____, and _____ . (Matthew 22:36-40; Mark 12:30)

28. Our lives are in order when they are permeated with _____.

29. God will not accept a cold, _____, _____, kind of love.

30. Godly thoughts provoked by the Holy Spirit produce _____.

31. The love we experience with God is to be lavished on our _____.

32. God expects us to love Him and our _____.

CHAPTER 13
GOD KNOWS US

1. What was Moses's failing?

2. What was David's propensity?

3. What was Solomon's weakness?

4. What was Jonah's prejudice?

5. What was Samson's defect?

6. What was Peter's misplaced confidence?

7. What was Saul's surprise?

8. The estimate we have of ourselves is _____,
   _____, and _____.

9. Why does nothing escape God?

10. God knows the beginning from the.

11. God knows us _____, _____, and perfectly.

12. What was Paul's dilemma in Romans 7:19?

13. God can warn _____ about _____ and save _____ from.

14. God knows us so well that He has all the hairs on our head.

15. After the Fall in the Garden of Eden, man became _____, _____, and *finite creatures*.

16. Does God know us before there is an *us*? (Jeremiah 1:15)

17. What does Psalm 139:4 reveal about God's knowledge?

18. Unlike man, God does not need _____, _____, _____, and _____ to know the heart of Man.

19. God is "a discerner of the thoughts and _____ of the heart." (Hebrew 4:12)

20. Thinking moves a person to _____. (Proverbs 23:7)

21. Whom was Ezekiel speaking to when he spoke these words: "For I know the things that come into your mind, every one of them"? (Ezekiel 11:5 NIV)

22. What is the warning in Matthew 12:36-37?

23. What is man's first and greatest need?

24. In John 10:27-30, what characterizes the relationship between the Shepherd and the sheep?

25. According to Ephesians 1, what has God done for us?

CHAPTER 14

ARE YOU LISTENING?

1. What methods are used to impart/teach information?

2. Life lessons do not have to be _____ , _____, or applied.

3. "Faith cometh by _____, and _____ by the Word of God."

4. James commanded that we "Be not hearers only" but also be "_____ the word." (James 1:22)

5. To grow in grace, love, and faith, we must _____ as recorded in His Word.

6. To hear the Word and not obey it is _____ and
    _____.

7. The Parable of the Sower identifies the kind of _____
    into which the seed, _____ is sown.

8. What are the four kinds of soils (hearts) onto which the Word
    of God falls?

9. What can cause our hearts to be hardened to the Word of God?

10. Who "snatches away the seed" sown in a *hardened heart*?

11. The *stony heart* is characterized by a lack of depth, and with
    no substantial root system, the Word of God is easily away.

12. *Thorny hearts* are choked by _____.

13. List some of the cares of this world.

14. What must we do to avoid being trapped by the cares of the
    world? (Romans 12:1-2; Matthew 6:33)

15. A seed received ought to be a seed that _____.

16. The ground of a heart that *hears,* *understands,* and *produces*
    is ground.

17. Connected to the Vine—Jesus Christ—we are expected to "

    _____."

18. Are believers expected to produce at the same level?

19. What do you think is your level of production? (thirty, sixty, hundredfold)

CHAPTER 15
DO YOUR JOB

1. What was Paul's advice to young Timothy?

2. Why was young Timothy warned to *do his job*?

3. Timothy was told that the Bosses, God the Father and God the Son, were watching him _____ his office.

4. As good stewards of God, we are not to give in to _____ behavior. (Romans 12:11, Hebrews 6:12a)

5. When Jesus returns to judge the world and set up His kingdom, man will have to stand before Him and give a _____ accounting.

6. No pastor can lead the church the _____ he wants without _____.

7. What did God promise to do to the pastors of Jeremiah's day who abused the sheep?

8. Timothy's primary job description was to _____.

9. The urgency of preaching meant that Timothy must always be and always look for opportunities to share the _____.

10. There is _____ in the Word of God. There is _____ in the Word of God and man needs _____.

11. Match the following heralders of the Word with their descriptions:

Paul	A. Preached good tidings unto the meek
Noah	B. The Pentecost preacher
James	C. A preacher who taught the words of truth
Phillip	D. The premier example
Isaiah	E. The leader of the early church
David	F. Preacher of righteousness
Peter	G. The planter of churches
John	H. The evangelist
Jesus	I. Preached righteousness in the great congregation
Solomon	J. The Revelator

12. Timothy was to be prepared to preach whether he _____ liked it or not, whether he _____ to or not.

13. The Word of God is always in _____; it is never _____. It speaks to all situations for all _____.

14. Define *reprove*.

15. How did Jesus reprove the scribes and the Pharisees who brought to Him a woman caught in adultery?

16. Define *rebuke*.

17. What weight was Timothy to set upon the people in hope that they would change?

18. What disciple did Jesus have to rebuke? What did Jesus say to him? (Matthew 16:21-23)

19. Define *exhort*.

20. Timothy's message to the people was to be a message of encouragement. _____ must never be the only message to the people.

21. Timothy was to carry out his preaching duty with all and _____.

22. When positive change among church members was slow, Timothy was to be _____ with them.

23. How did Paul address the urgency of Timothy's job? (2 Timothy 4:3)

24. Paul warned Timothy (and the church) of a time when men would rather hear everything except the _____.

25. From the "litany of evil characteristics" found in 2 Timothy 3:2-4, which ones are seemingly more prominent today?

26. What is meant by *itching ears*? (2 Timothy 4:3)

27. In Jeremiah 3:15, what kind of pastors/teachers did God promise His church?

28. To deny Jesus Christ as God, "The way, the truth, and the life," is to deny _____, _____, and the for the atonement of sins.

29. In place of God's Word, to what other avenues have people gleefully subscribed?

30. In concluding his letter to Timothy, what four admonitions did Paul give Timothy that would assure success in and out of the pulpit? (2 Timothy 4:5)

31. What are the action words in 2 Timothy 4:5?

32. Although evil may appear to be triumphant, what will be the conclusion of the matter? (See Psalm 37:1-2)

33. Persecution of the saint is inevitable. However, what has God promised in Psalm 34:19?

34. Every preacher must endure the _____, _____, and the _____ by members and non-members.

35. Match the following examples of enduring persecution:

John the Baptist   A. Beaten and thrown in prison

Moses   B. The Chief Sufferer

Joseph   C. Thrown into the lion's den

Jeremiah   D. Endured the murmuring of his people

Jesus   E. Suffered at the hands of his brothers

Daniel   F. Beheaded for his preaching

36. Doing the work of an evangelist will help to ward off teachers and _____ clergy.

37. If Timothy performed his duties by teaching and preaching to the best of his ability, what would be the result?

CHAPTER 16
THE CHALLENGE: GO ON AND DO IT

1. 1 Corinthians 15 is often referred to as the _____.

2. We have victory over death through _____.
    (1 Corinthians 15:57)

3. What was the result of Paul preaching to the Corinthians? (1 Corinthians 1:4)

4. How many witnessed the appearances of the resurrected Lord? (1 Corinthians 15:5-7)

5. Where did Paul experience the resurrected Lord? (1 Corinthians 15:8; Acts 9)

6. List those who spoke out against the resurrection.

7. What was the purpose of the seven greatest "ifs" in the Bible, as found in 1 Corinthians 15:12-19 NIV?

8. In 1 Corinthians 15:35 through 15:57, Paul provides what four divisions that further explain and defend the resurrection?

    a. _____

    b. _____

    c. _____

    d. _____

9. Christ's ultimate victory over death must serve as the _____, and _____ of the Christian life.

10. Accepting by faith what Jesus did on Calvary will determine whether we as believers can "_____."

11. Paul, facing much persecution and hostility, made what confident declaration in the resurrected Lord? (2 Timothy 1:12)

12. Because of man's lack of belief in the resurrected Lord, attempts have been made, with some success, to remove the _____that have made us a favorable people in the eyes of God.

13. What are some of those landmarks?

14. What will it take to endure the storms of disobedience and defiance that grip the world today?

15. What inspires and motivates a believer to continue his or her work for God?

16. Our work for the Lord must be built on the _____ that is laid in _____.

17. When we build on the foundation Christ has laid, then our labor for the Master is never in _____.

18. The God of Love will _____ our labor of _____. (Revelation 22:12)

OTHER BOOKS

Is It True?

Lie after Lie after Lie

From the Pulpit to the Streets

www.ingramcontent.com/pod-product-compliance
Lightning Source LLC
Chambersburg PA
CBHW050904120626
46554CB00003B/1010